ɔr before

Parents Orators Writers Artists Readers

P.o.w.a.r

A Family Learning Project

Other books from the Powar series include the Intermediate Reader, 'Weeding Cane', the Beginner Reader, 'Learn to Listen, Then You Won't Feel' and the anthology 'Our Say'. Please check the back of this book for details of the Powar Poster Collection.

The Power From Within

Parents rapping about life, parenthood and their children

NATIONAL
LOTTERY
CHARITIES
BOARD

Powar Project Co-ordinator, Leroy Williamson
Crèche Co-ordinator, Elizabeth Aryee
Text copyright © Anita Allen, Elizabeth Henry, Sonia Hughes, Paulette Martin. 2001
Editor, Leroy Williamson
Illustrations, Ian Bobb
Design, Ian Bobb and Leroy Williamson

Published & distributed by Gatehouse Books Ltd.
Hulme Adult Education Centre, Stretford Road, Manchester M15 5FQ.
Printed by RAP Ltd, Clock Street, Hollinwood, Oldham, OL9 7LY
ISBN 0 906253 91 8
British Library cataloguing in publication data:
A catalogue record for this book is available from the British Library

'The Power From Within' was developed from writing originally produced by Anita Allen,
Elizabeth Henry, Sonia Hughes and Paulette Martin with editor, Leroy Williamson.
The writing was drawn from workshops during the Powar family learning project at
Claremont Infant School, Moss Side, Manchester.

One Gatehouse reading circle recommended these stories for publication. Many
thanks for their work to Steph Prior, Sonia Hammond, Susan Armstrong, Wendy
Gibbons, Monica Ebanks and Joseph Campbell.

Thanks also to the English and Basic Skills groups run by Manchester Adult Education
Services at Ducie Adult Education Centre and Greenheys Adult Education Centre with
whom we piloted a first draft of this book.

Special thanks also to Judy Craven, Sonia Hammond, Ruth Nunes, Harvey Nisbett and
Pat Lee who were instrumental to the success of the project.

Gatehouse acknowledges grant aid towards the production of this book from The
National Lottery and Manchester City Council.

Gatehouse is a member of The Federation of Worker Writers & Community Publishers.

Gatehouse provides an opportunity for writers to express their thoughts and feelings
on aspects of their lives. The views expressed are not necessarily those of Gatehouse.

Contents

Preface

Family Literacy

Family literacy is all about parents and children learning together and from each other, given that parents are the first and most important teachers a child can have. Family literacy programmes aim to create awareness amongst parents of how and what children are taught within school. They also demonstrate ways in which parents can help their child with reading and writing and in turn gain confidence with their own literacy skills.

Parental support is key to the success or failure of many of our children. Especially in a growing climate of high exclusion rates, limited resources, big class sizes and intense social and peer pressures.

Powar   *P.arents O.rators W.riters A.rtists R.eaders*

The Powar Family Learning Project was launched at Claremont Infant School, Moss Side Manchester in 1999 Its aim was to deliver a programme that would benefit parents of children of African descent. A key objective is to encourage parents to express themselves. Powar aims to empower by developing parents' talents as orators, writers, artists and readers. The writing in this book represents the first fruits of this labour.

This and the accompanying books in the Powar Series have been drawn from a parents' writing group at Claremont Infant School. We met for weekly workshops for over a year. Workshops used an African and African-Caribbean cultural perspective at its core and included sessions on oral story telling, music therapy, puppet making and black literature. These workshops were complemented by sessions on school procedures, the National Curriculum and practical support activities that could be done at home with children.

The Writing

The other half of the project involved getting parents to write. As editor of the project, it was my job to encourage parents to write. Many of the parents had not written anything creative for a long time, since school, for some. Subsequently, confidence and self-belief to express in their own voice was lacking at the beginning. However, after the first workshops, the parents grew to know each other quite well. We gained each other's trust and respect and gelled together as a group. Sometimes it was like sitting in the midst of long lost sisters who had just been reunited and had a lot of catching up to do.

Early on, we found that a good method to extract writing from the group was first to have a discussion workshop about an issue or opinion. All workshops were tape recorded and then transcribed. The transcribed notes were then presented to the parents with suggestions and advice on how to complete a writing exercise.

In these early sessions, we talked, debated and reasoned about issues related to being a parent and being a parent of a black child. We covered a range of issues such as concepts of freedom, identity, role models, fears and hopes and parenting values. The wealth of writing that came from this approach was inspired first and foremost by the children. The children more than anything else were the driving force behind the parents' writing. However, I feel that if the parents were not given time and space to express themselves orally in the first instance, then the richness and honesty of the writing may not have shone through like it does.

For myself as the co-ordinator and editor of the project the time spent with the group has been enjoyable, rewarding, testing but above all, an enlightening adventure.

So therefore, maximum respect to the writers - Anita Allen, Paulette Martin, Sonia Hughes and Elizabeth Henry. And also to their children and grandchildren who kept us all on our toes - Solomon, Erika and Jaimeel, Luke and Isaac, Nathanael and Kerith.

What makes this collection of writing so special is that each parent offers a distinctive and original voice but all seem to connect at the same root. The writing therefore may hold a special meaning for everybody, if not only for parents. We hope you enjoy reading the books and trust you will be able to take something positive from them.

Leroy Williamson
(Editor)

Introduction

This book was written with much dedication by some of the parents and carers of children who attend Claremont Infant School. Parents have displayed their dedication in many, many ways, particularly to their children, so it isn't surprising to see that they could produce such quality literature.

Patricia Lee, Head Teacher, and Ruth Nunes, a teacher at the school who supports families of African descent, have endeavoured over the years to involve parents at every level of their children's education. They believe that parents are the real experts. Leroy Williamson, the project co-ordinator, has shown strength of spirit and has encouraged the women in the group, inspiring and helping to build the confidence required to realise their full potential.

As a child, I often heard the saying, 'women are the weaker sex.' But this, as the years have passed, has proved to be more and more untrue. Weakness and strength like many others words can be defined in a million different ways by a million different people. On reaching adulthood I began to realise that we can only reach true definitions when we base them on what we have within. Only when we look within, do we find real truth and meaning in the outside world. Parents, on the whole, pass on to their children the values and survival skills that they feel their children should possess. They know that we all have to look into ourselves, at what we have been given, to make sense of our world. Mothers and fathers both play their roles in this process in their own unique but yet similar ways. As far as I have experienced, women have shown themselves to be capable of directing the play of life with a show of strength beyond measure.

The women who created this amazing writing set out at the beginning to keep it real. They have written of their hopes, dreams, fears, loves and hates, candidly, which will surely move the soul of anyone who reads. Freedom and security for their children is one of the themes running through these pieces. Look beyond the surface and see how women through the ages past, present and future have held these concerns close to their hearts, weaving those concepts into their active lives.

Reading this book and other books in the Powar series involves the reader viewing life from a range of experiences, through the eyes of a child, sister, partner or wife and mother. The authors have succeeded in producing something that can be felt, seen with the mind's eye and almost touched. The power of this literature is such that the experiences of these parents become 'real' and meaningful to readers of any background.

Harvey Nisbett
(Local teacher who works with ethnic minority
children at Claremont School)

Freedom and Security

What does freedom and security mean to you? How do you define freedom? Are you free? Are your children free? Is your freedom and security hindered by the place you live, where you work, the colour of your skin or how much money you make? Or does your sense of freedom and security come from within? Maybe in reality both your freedom and security are controlled by others? Is education part of the key to feeling free and secure?

Discussing freedom and security is a very emotive subject. However when looking at the concept when applied to children from a parents point of view, it becomes supercharged. As parents we all want the best for our children.

Freedom Is Having a Choice

by Elizabeth Henry

Freedom Is Having A Choice

The words *freedom* and *security* can be described in many ways for everyone has their own criteria with which to make the definition. Many only base this on what they can perceive in the physical life. If I were to do the same, then my conclusion would be that I have neither.

At this moment in time, the freedom and security of both my children and myself have been taken away by one man. He has on numerous occasions threatened to take my life. I cannot dismiss this threat, as it has been made by a person who has no regard for others. He will lie in wait and strike when the opportunity is given to him. So I constantly look over my shoulder. Sitting in the park with my children is not the happy scene it may appear to an observer, as I constantly watch. Within what should be the secure atmosphere of our home, I know that windows and doors, even when locked, can be no defence.

When I was living in a relationship where profanity and violence were more abundant than compassion and respect, I knew that I had one freedom left, that of choice. Too many people stay in an abusive situation because it is the easiest option. I did not choose to depart from that existence for myself. My opinion of my own self-worth had been so totally destroyed that I did not fit into any equation. My children did not deserve to grow up being indoctrinated into a life of hypocrisy and violence.

My lifestyle has been altered.

Yes, I do live in constant fear that I may be separated or taken from my children. I cannot always go where, or do what I would like, so I choose to do something else.

No, I do not have money in excess, however I have enough to feed and clothe my children. Why should my family gorge themselves on materialistic ideals while others starve?

Just as ivy smothers a plant
you entangled your malevolence,
trying to conquer and control.
With my last ounce of strength
I took us from your clutches.

Now I live the life of the hunted.

Scared of noises and shadows,
fearing knocks at the door.
But unlike a rabbit in the headlights
I did not stand waiting for the kill,
for I knew there was a better life.

And every day I pray
for strength and guidance to protect us,
because I face each day
knowing that in the shadows you hide,
plotting and scheming
my demise.

Freedom of choice is something that is available on all levels of existence and can be a powerful force. An oppressed person can choose to capitulate or fight for what is right. The fight does not have to be physical. If they hold strong to what they believe is just, they can become free. Many times I have heard and read the phrase *Freedom is a state of mind.* I believe that we all have to deal with a physical level of existence. Some become so enmeshed with this that they lose sight of what is truly important and what is the greatest source of freedom and security.

I find it very hard to understand people who have no spiritual faith. Those who believe their lives revolve around materialism, base their worth on houses, cars and a bank balance. They would base freedom on where they can go and the law of the land. Security would be how good their locks and alarms are and if they have more than enough money for their lifestyle.

If they looked at me, they would most likely say that I am poor, that I have no freedom or security. That is how I see them. For in reality I know that I have an abundance of both because I am strong internally and neither man, woman nor beast can take that from me.

The Pavo from Within

by Anita Allen

The Power From Within

Freedom: *Being not in bondage or under restraint. The power of self determination. Having no obligation. Frankness.*

There is a calypso song that says,

Freedom we go march in peace,
We no 'fraid police.
Politicians could go to hell,
For we want freedom for
Our black brothers in South Africa and Angola.

Even though the world is crying, praying and preaching for freedom, do we really know what to do with it when we get it?

Freedom is a way of life we all crave. Not many are able to handle being free. Being downtrodden and miseducated for many years, many of us suffer from a hereditary problem that shows itself in the way we think. It's like even for a split second we can't get by without somebody's help.

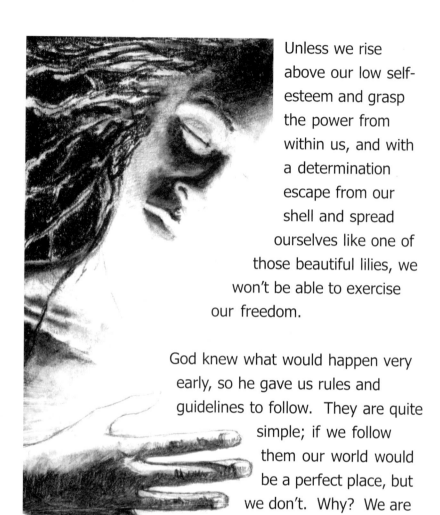

Unless we rise above our low self-esteem and grasp the power from within us, and with a determination escape from our shell and spread ourselves like one of those beautiful lilies, we won't be able to exercise our freedom.

God knew what would happen very early, so he gave us rules and guidelines to follow. They are quite simple; if we follow them our world would be a perfect place, but we don't. Why? We are so free, so free that we just do as we please. Do we really know what to do with freedom? Or do we always want a Massa or a Missis over us? No we don't. Many of us were born in sad times, bad times, difficult times. We have inherited some very bad blood.

22

Some have tried, some would try, and we will always try to be free!

*F*eeling that comes from deep within so our outward lives can portray what we feel.

*R*ally around our family and friends so that they can be strong.

*E*ndurance, for suffering with patience and fortitude

*E*vidence of achievement.

*D*etermination to reach our destiny.

*O*neness in which we should fight.

*M*iseducation to education; to becoming scientists, record breakers, T.V producers and any other thing we so choose to accomplish.

History and Identity

Carter G. Woodson, who founded Black History Month, tells us that,

> 'Every person has two educations: that which is given to them, and the other which he or she gives to themselves. Of the two kinds the second is by far the more desirable. Indeed, all that is most worthy in a person, you must work out and conquer for yourselves. It is that which constitutes our real and best nourishment.
>
> What we are merely taught seldom nourishes the mind like that which we teach ourselves.'

We as parents are responsible for the understanding our children have of who they are and their place in the world.

Bass lines

by Sonia Hughes

Bass Lines

I don't know about my history
I understand certain bad things happened
I believe we did great things
I have no proof, I have no dates
I feel my history.

But histories, apparently, must be written. They should be verified and evidenced, documented and artefacted, tested and proved, agreed and acknowledged. I have none of these. Before I can deal you the facts, and you will need these, I will have to dig for myself.

I must unearth my roots and inspect the links. I must trace and outline, note and learn. For now I have to rely on my feeling.

But my historical feeling is not always strong. Sometimes I forget my long-linedness, my habit of survival, my rising up and excellence, my innovation, my beauty, my strength, my learning, my love.

Sometimes I forget and sometimes I choose not to know. I often ignore my trade in slaves, my appalling wars, my corruption, my life of crime, my madness, my collaboration, assimilation and denial.

How do I come to forget? Is it the basics of the life I lead? That aside from those day to dailies of work and survival, that I close my soul to what I am.

Modern life favours histories and identities free from contradiction or complexity but that is my history as I feel it. But still sometimes I forget.

Then something unstoppable makes me remember.

A deep, deep song, a rhythm, a dance, a collection of people, a princess, a dark, dark handsome prince and then

I remember. And I wonder how I could have ever forgot. Forgotten, that I am from the soil, that the dances that I weave are deep, deep from long ago, from unknown forbears, who danced these dances. And I feel their steps as they guide me through the rhythms of people who probably never forget and are always at one with who they are.

And then I remember the last time I was there, when I knew what it was to be whole, when I had that sense of home inside me.

And so there I am, I'm on this no-nation tip, and a bass-line, hard, shaking, slippery, sex-full plays, and I don't just hear it, me and the bass-line connect and I'm earthed, grounded, founded, recall things that had slipped my mind, find my way back.

I am at once ashamed and relieved and unbelieving that this knowing, this heartbeat, this sense of me, my past, my identity, my history had ever left me.

But that's my historical feeling. The artefacts and evidence elude me. They are out there and I should know them intimately, boast and brag about them, be able to produce them to prove a point. Use the dates to illustrate the truth.

But I cannot and I recognise it is dangerous to be unarmed in alien territory. And as my historical feeling is unreliable, if I should suffer an attack, I would be unable to defend myself but for the sheer force of historical feeling which I hope would rise up and blast my assailant!

.

Walking Bricks

by Elizabeth Henry

Talking Bricks

Three minibuses left Claremont School bound for the
Liverpool Maritime Museum. Specifically, we were going
to the part of the museum called the Slavery Gallery.
I was going because I wanted to open my children's minds,
to let them see what had transpired when slavery was to
many an accepted part of life.

Inside the museum we were given a short talk on the
gallery. We were allowed to handle some of the artefacts
such as manacles and the punishment collar. These were
forged from metal and used to control the enslaved
people.

We met Eric who was a guide for the museum. After
lunch he was going to take us round the streets of
Liverpool to point out the evidence laid in stone that
linked Liverpool with transatlantic slavery.

The gallery was full of displays, even telephones that give
audio information on the slave trade between the fifteenth
and eighteenth centuries. It was too much to absorb in
one visit. We sat outside eating lunch with the view of the
ships and boats. Then it was time for our tour of the

streets of Liverpool.

Eric stood before the group and introduced himself.
"I'm a Black Liverpudlian and I get really annoyed when
people say that Liverpool did not prosper from the slave
trade."
We stopped at the cold grey waters of the Mersey and Eric
said,
"I don't do dates."

His idea was, he gets you interested with the visual story
and then you can look up the dates. I liked that, I wanted
a lesson in history not a history lesson.

He told us about the different industries along the Mersey;
ship building for trade and the cocoa to Cadburys to make
chocolate. In the 1600's cafes were chocolate houses.
I was enjoying this and even the children were taking
notice of this man. He certainly knew his stuff!

He painted a picture of Liverpool way back when the
Mersey was wider and the first hints of a town sprung up.
The stench of the streets filled the area known as L1.
Liverpool 1. The origins of the modern city.

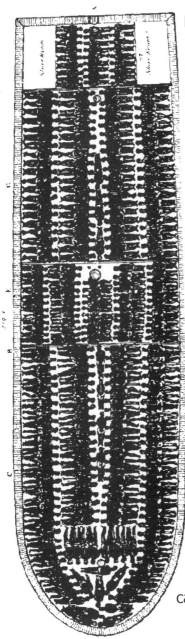

Now we were about to see the language that buildings talk. As Eric said, when you walk, look up and see what they have to say. The designs etched into their bricks are a concrete history lesson. After a few pointers, those *talking bricks* and our group were communicating just fine. They spoke of the slave ships, the chains, dolphins, the Lion of England, the Eagle of America, faces of all nations, Neptune the god of the sea.

Eric also told us of the French prisoners of war who built parts of the docks and the statue that depicts them in Exchange Flags, a small business area in Liverpool. Here, traders used to shake hands on deals, buying and selling their ships' cargo: cotton, tobacco, rice and sugar cane. Slave crops.

Money became abundant. Banks formed and prospered. The doorway of Barclays Bank shows Neptune with his hands on the heads of two black children holding gold bags. On their wrists and ankles you can see the bands of slavery.

Liverpool might not have brought in vast numbers of slaves to its own shores to be sold to the highest bidder yet it was certainly built on the blood of slaves.

The triangular trade brought the wealth to Liverpool to make it what it is today. History cannot be forgotten, it should not be forgotten. In Liverpool there is a constant reminder of where and what the city spawned - the slave trade.

The talking bricks do not just tell the tale, they shout it loud and clear. We will not forget now that Eric has translated and taught us their language. Go and see for yourself. *Look, Listen and Learn.*

Keeping Our Culture Alive In Our kids

by Anita Allen

Keeping Our Culture Alive In Our Kids

Our ancestors came all the way from Africa to the western world as slaves and the only thing they brought and kept was their culture. We left our homeland Montserrat because of the ongoing volcanic crisis. We came away from the ash and stress. It is most important and it is also our duty to keep our culture alive in our kids.

A History

Many years ago Christopher Columbus persuaded the king and queen of Spain to give him some ships so he could explore and make them rich. Many thought the world was flat but his dreams told him differently. So with three ships and some men he set sail. On his second voyage on November 11th 1492, he spotted an island. Although the Spanish never occupied the island they changed its name from the Amerindian *Alleouagana* to *Santa Maria de Montserrat.* Columbus named the island in honour of a mountain abbey outside Barcelona.

The Amerindians were the people who occupied the islands before. They travelled in canoes, which they carved from huge trees and they ate seeds or fruits. Some of them were known cannibals. Some, like the Arawaks lived close to the seashores and some, like the Caribs lived in the mountains. Some Caribs are still known to be in places like Dominica and St. Lucia.

The British controlled Montserrat in 1632. About this time Thomas Warner settled on the island with a group of Irish Roman Catholics who were in search of unmolested altars. In those days Christians were staked and burned at the altars, so they were looking for clean ones. Between 1665 and 1805 the island was invaded at least six times by either the British or the French.

The Irish Legacy

The Irish brought names of people and places to the island. Places and names such as Patrick, Kinsale, Irish, Galloway and Ryan. There is still uncertainty about the detail and precise nature of their legacy, but they brought more than just names. They brought Roman Catholicism to the island. They also may have provided the ingredients for the recipe of goat water, our island's national dish, and have influenced Creole music.

The African Legacy

Our biggest ethnic element in the Montserratian culture is African. The importation of Africans started in the late 1640's and they quickly outnumbered the whites. From 523 Africans in 1672, the number grew to over 6400 at emancipation. As their number grew the whites dwindled. A kind of apartheid existed between whites and the vast majority of Africans.

Two cultures virtually existed on the plantation. Apart from occasional sexual liaison, what really united blacks and whites was English. The language of the cane piece. Africans were forced to suppress their native languages and learn the language of production, so whites and Africans were somewhat bonded through English rooted in Montserratian soil.

Montserratian Creole is a fusion of African languages and English. It adds colour and a unique flavour to our island speech and culture. *Ge me le wha yah yet da*[1], *Teck um up han um gi me*[2], *Ah gel a wha de, Chrismus a do fu u*[3]? That's the Montserratian way.

---

[1] Give me a little of what you're eating.
[2] Take it up and give it to me.
[3] Girl, what is the Christmas doing for you?

British Legacy

From the English we adopt Westminster-style parliamentary democracy and some of their holidays and ceremonies. Although the island was settled by Irish Catholics, it was Anglicanism that was the dominant religion. Our first church, St. Anthony's was situated in the capital, Plymouth. Early June is the Queen's official birthday. The governor who represents the Queen arrives in ceremonial dress and inspects a guard of honour consisting of local forces.

Emancipation and Celebration

St. Patrick's Day celebration forms a key memorial to the Irish. In Montserrat it is much more than a holy feast day. For on March 17th 1768, choosing the day strategically, the African slaves planned to overthrow their planter-lords and win their freedom by force of arms. The plot was uncovered and the organisers were murdered, but they are celebrated annually since 1985, as our unnamed heroes and freedom fighters.

Although we celebrate a rebellion, the focus is not on pageantry and prominent people in our history. The shamrock is often depicted as an emblem of our freedom from slavery. We celebrate Labourers' Day and Whitsuntide and Easter.

The slaves in Montserrat were disappointed when on August 1st 1834 they did not get full emancipation. Nevertheless, many attended church services. On August 1st 1838 they had their day and for decades after, they celebrated the anniversary of real emancipation with song, dance and merriment.

Fir's o' August come again
Hurrah for Nincum Riley
Buckra[4] bit me, I bit him back
Hurrah for Nincum Riley

Nincum Riley was a literate slave who, according to oral tradition, read the emancipation proclamation to some of his colleagues.

We celebrate Christmas on Montserrat for eight days. In this time African culture explodes. However, during slavery, only three days were allotted for Christmas celebration, which featured drums, music, ritual dances and folk religion, some of which have survived in the masquerades.

---

[4] A word commonly used to describe white people or Europeans.

Now it's queenshows, calypso, steel pan, hi-fi music and revelry which all climax on New Years Day. All troops, groups, bands, kings and queens and everyone who is colourfully dressed, parade the streets, prancing, dancing, whining and railing back to back.

No matter what happens from here onward, this is the way I'll always keep my culture alive in my kids and grandkids.

Christmas Come

Drums pounding
Men and women dancing
Like mask mummies
Colourfully dressed
Voices shouting
Ladies strain
Whips cracking
Pennies falling
Masquerades shuffling
As they dance from sun up to sun set
Dancing, celebrating
'cause Christmas come

Quarter pound crown cheese
Turn-over-tart, three sided cake
Rice pudding, cassava bread
Rum, all kind of rum
Cockspur, vodka, brandy, gin
Perk's punch and even soda water
Set de jumbie[5] table ma
Christmas come

---

[5] A ghost or spirit.

Carol singing all night long
Silent night, while shepherd watch flocks
Men wonder how far from Bethlehem they came
Wise men carry gifts
While children waiting to open them
Revellers dancing, children sleeping
Then shouting, laughing, tears and rejoicing
'cause Christmas come.

Identity

by Paulette Martin

Identity?

African heritage
Born in Lewisham
Raised in Manchester
Saw my colour - degraded
Reflected in TV and media
Go to conferences, to upgrade me?
To confirm the colour I am?....but

Why do I have to say I'm black?

First no knowledge of past histories;
Yet I wasn't denying that we've been through pain,
My parents denied the ability to strive.
As second class citizens invited over to rest as a first class
person
To work for society whose deity was based on the fact that
their colour was too much.
And this... is as far as it goes.

Why do they have to be afraid to be black?

I've come up saying, "I want to be equal" but not
pointing to my colour, just my being as an individual.

I've battled with looks when I walk down the street with white people I know.
Being told, "Why can't you go out with a black guy?"

I say, "Why don't they go out with **ME**?"

Why do they make what I do a shame, a disgrace?
Because the man beside me is not my colour or race.
Why do some black men see me as a nothing?
Unless I stand by their side making integration
"Not right."

Afterword

Looking back at *'Identity'* which was written in the early eighties, the issues brought up still exist although maybe not as prevalently or as obviously. Marriage has brought me closer to people of my own culture and is doubly reinforced within my faith, as the church I attend is predominately black.

Twenty years ago I was mixing with people of all races. I was working in the environment of the arts (music and theatre), all of which at that time were predominately Caucasian owned or regulated.

Now TV and media reflect black people and their part in society a little more equally. A good example is the recent acknowledgement in a television documentary, which looked at the West Indian Regiment, their active involvement in the First World War and their subsequent mistreatment.

Whilst I no longer work in the arts and now work in a caring profession, I still see inequality, although now I tend to strive for the rights of the disabled, specifically the deaf. The deaf appear to have no place in society and therefore no say. They use a language, which whilst beautiful to me is still in some ways ignored.

I do believe my poem spoke correctly of how I felt as a black woman then. However, the older I have become, the more I realise I still wish to integrate even more on all levels and not necessarily on the issue of race only.

Respect

The word inspire comes from the Greek,` to breathe life into.' The word hero derives from the word `heru' which in ancient kemetic (Egyptian) means `saviour'. Is there a special person in your life or an important figure from the past that has inspired you?

Heroes and heroines come from all walks of life. Our personal heroes have often earned respect and admiration through their actions. It's important, especially for children to have positive role models that they can relate to and identify with. Guidance and direction in life often comes from those you respect.

The Hero In My Life

by Paulette Martin

The Hero in My Life

When asked, "Who is your hero?" I immediately thought I
have no heroes, as I have never knowingly adored
someone in such a way. As a Christian my faith would
never allow me to put another human being above it.

If you were to ask me to pick someone on a human level
it would have to be my husband. To me, he's my prince
and he always makes me feel like his princess. We've
been through the same life experiences and balance each
other out completely. However it is difficult to explain just
how much of a hero he is because it's a personal thing.

The word *hero* also supposes that
they are super human and they
are far superior to anyone.
I would much prefer to
say I admire a person and
the qualities they either
have, or have passed on
during their life. In this
way I can name the
following people as those I
have admired or reflect an ideology

57

I wish to attain.

Martin Luther King, a preacher and a forerunner of racial integration, I named my hero. He believed every man, woman, and child should have equal access to all and every public amenity under God given laws. His stand secured the right for black boys and girls to attend any high school, as opposed to segregated ones.

Rosa Park's refusal to give up her seat because a Caucasian

person needed to sit down fuelled the Montgomery Bus Boycott. Her actions make her a heroine in my eyes because she demanded the right to not be treated anything less than a human being. Martin Luther King took up her cause, encouraging black people who travelled by bus to stop using them until the law was changed.

In doing this, a sense of self worth grew among the black and indigenous peoples and an awareness of discrimination amongst the Caucasians. Martin Luther King epitomised for me equality and anti-discrimination. He, however was only following one who is truly my hero, namely Jesus Christ.

His life is a perfect example of helping others. He made friends with those who would never have a friend. He healed those that were sick. He taught about loving one another as you would wish to be loved, whether a stranger, enemy or friend. He never judged or criticised. While this would seem impossible to achieve, Jesus to me is an excellent example of a hero. He can do all things and nothing is impossible to him.

No Contest

by Elizabeth Mary

No Contest

Heroism to me is not the empty grand gesture. It is something that shows inner strength, modesty and humility, whether intentional or not. There are people today who demand respect and those who try to buy it. Yet in reality it has to be earned.

Dictators send out their armies to murder and destroy the lives of the people they are supposed to protect. Simon Weston was horrifically maimed in the Falklands War.

Did he seek vengeance?

No.

He forgave the pilot that sent the missile. He rebuilt his life and is now helping others.

Who is the hero?

A millionaire gives a few thousand pounds to charity. A grand gesture! Many will sing his praises. Lenny Henry and Roy Castle are just two people who could have done the same yet they chose to be different.

Roy Castle campaigned tirelessly to raise funds for a special cancer hospital until he passed away. Lenny Henry goes and sees firsthand the problems some endure. They both give more than money. A small child gives a week's pocket money to charity.

The person who literally lives hand to mouth gives a few pounds to someone who is destitute. It is not how much that you give financially that matters, it is what you feel when you give it.

Tell me who are your heroes?

There are people who suffer seemingly insurmountable difficulties every day yet they never give up hope.

My friend has cancer. She also has her only son wrongly incarcerated, yet she never puts her troubles before those of others. She is a second 'Mum' to so many I have lost count. Another close friend suffers severe mental problems, constantly tormented, yet he always makes others laugh. He has genuine concern for others and their well being.

Are they not heroes?

No Contest

The Strap

by Anita Allen.

The Strap

I was born in our only hospital, the Glendon Hospital, in the capital, Plymouth, on the island of Montserrat. My parents were from St. John's, in the far north of my island. I have three brothers and two sisters by my mother and two sisters and two brothers by my father. As a child I never knew them, I only knew about them.

I was given away to a family in Salem, which is in the centre of the island. The only family member I knew was my father, and after I had my kids we became friends. I accepted him for who he was. The first time I saw my mother or ever remember seeing her face was 1976. She is okay and I call her Miss Sarah. I can't remember a thing before I went to school at the age of five.

I knew I was very happy to go to school, but when I got there it was a nightmare. I was given a slate and a pencil to write with. I am left-handed. My teacher couldn't stand me being left-handed so she always beat me on my knuckles. I seldom went out for breaks because my work was never finished. I knew I hated her but I had no one to tell. In spite of being left-handed, I tried very hard to do the best I could. I was determined to get a good job and go far away from home.

I felt very alone and mistreated. I did everything. Even going to the pasture which was very far away, to bring the milk from the cows. I would then bottle it out and carry it to the neighbour's house. I would fill all the buckets and jars in the house with water, and then I had to take the sheep and goats to nearby places to feed. I had to do all of this before going to school at nine o'clock. Then I would run along to school barefoot. At lunchtime I would carry water to the nearby animals before going back to school on the hot pitch road.

I am older now and when I look back, I can joke about it and feel happy. I've survived and have the love and support of my children, and some of my brothers and sisters that I've come to know and love.

In school I never paid much attention to my teachers though I passed through a lot of them. I wanted what they had, so all that really mattered to me was doing my best and getting good marks. I remember getting really mad if anyone got more than me and tried to see how they got it. So having a special teacher wasn't my thing. Now I have time to think back, smilingly, I'd recommend Mr. Charles Willock, our head teacher.

Mr. Willock came to our school when I was in third standard or grade 3. He was different from other headmasters. He was everybody's teacher. Back then people were classified as upper class, those who can afford anything; middle class were those above average and lower were those who could barely make two ends meet. But with Mr. Willock everybody was in the business to achieve and achieve we did.

He was very strict in everything, but it was late-coming
that he hated. He and his strap would often meet us
around the corners or he would hide behind hedges just
to see if we idled on the road. The strap was part of him.
The strap went everywhere that he went.

Mr. Willock turned our school around in every way. He made it possible for even the lower class children to gain entrance into grammar school (as it was called). He pushed us to learn. He gave lessons after and during school. I couldn't stay after, so I got my full share during class. Even though I didn't go to secondary school I knew it was not because of him, but I should have gone. He was instrumental in getting me into the Montserrat Commercial School, which is now the Technical College. So I guess that full tribute goes out to Mr. Charles Willock from me.

A few years ago I met him under different circumstances. He is now an ordained Anglican minister. He said, "Anita, the reason why I was on your case so much is because you were a very good student going places." He also said, "My only disappointment is that you didn't achieve what I wanted for you and what you really wanted for yourself," and that he was quite happy to have taught me.

I might not have reached my goals, whatever they were. However, I have come a long way and with my children and grandchildren by my side, I am very happy.

The Super Hero that Died

by Sonia Hughes

The Super Hero Who Died

I could talk about Nelson or Malcolm or Rosa or Winnie,
how I was knocked out by Ali or thrilled by Michael. But
as a child, it was my brother.

He was ten years older than me until he died. Now my big
brother will always be twenty-two while my life carries on.

Mum says when he was a baby and they first came to this
country, they lived in one room in Effra Road, Brixton.
She went to work and left him with a child minder and
when she came back from work he was in the same
nappy, soaking wet.

I have a picture of him and me. I'm wearing a dress with
a white lace bodice and a red velvet skirt. He's wearing a
suit; he's about twelve or thirteen. And I'm standing in
front of him, and he has his hands on my shoulders.

He had a small toy projector and you slid the slide in front
of the light. He used to give me film shows on the hall
wall with the lights turned out. He let me play with his
train set and sometimes we would play crocodiles in the
water.

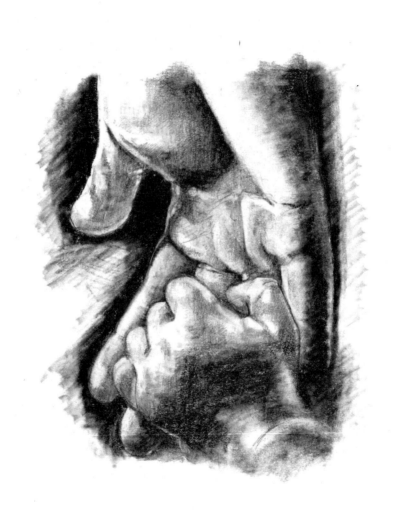

He had a table football game and in the summer all his dishy friends would come round and play in the front room. One day he and his friends went walking over the back across the building site and he took me with them. But I wet my navy blue knickers and he had to come back with me to the house and he didn't fuss.

I remember his spooner shoes[1] and my mum used to press his hair on Friday nights when he went to the California Ballroom. At New Year's parties, he was always the best dancer.

After he left school, he was in a band. They played all over the place. He had a Vauxhall Viva. The band wore satin tops. My brother wore sunglasses, the same shape as the Bionic Man's[2] sunglasses.

He let me stay with him and his mates in Torquay where the band had a summer residency. I was planning to tell him I loved him as I got on the coach. But I forgot to.

---

[1] Spooner shoes were fashionable in the late 1970's.

[2] The Bionic Man is a character from the 1970's T.V. series 'The Six Million Dollar Man'.

Set of 8 original full colour posters.
2 pack sizes available - A2 or A3
For an order form please call Gatehouse Books on
0161 226 7152.

The posters reflect positive images of mothers and their children. Writing produced by the parent complements each poster. The collection supports the belief that parents are the first and most important teachers of a child.

Positive images of parents and children of African descent are rare. These posters will document, inspire and promote the value of families learning together and from each other.

The term 'parent' in the above instance applies equally to a child's carer or guardian.

Gatehouse Books

Gatehouse is a unique publisher
Our writers are adults who are developing their basic
reading and writing skills. Their ideas and experiences
make fascinating material for any reader, but are
particularly relevant for adults working on their reading
and writing skills. The writing strikes a chord – a shared
experience of struggling against many odds.

The format of our books is clear and uncluttered. The
language is familiar and the text is often line-broken, so
that each line ends at a natural pause.

Gatehouse books are both popular and respected within
Adult Basic Education throughout the English speaking
world. They are also a valuable resource within
secondary schools, Social Services and within the Prison
Education Service and Probation Services.

Booklist available

Gatehouse Books
Hulme Adult Education Centre
Stretford Road
Manchester
M15 5FQ.
Tel and Fax: 0161 226 7152
E-mail: office@gatehousebooks.org.uk
Website: www.gatehousebooks.org.uk

The Gatehouse Publishing Charity Ltd is a registered charity, no 1011042
Gatehouse Books Ltd is a company limited by guarantee reg. no. 2619614